Helen Jeffery

Buckled

Salamander Street

PLAYS

First published in 2026 by Salamander Street Ltd., a Wordville imprint. (info@salamanderstreet.com).

Cover image by pixabay.com

ISBN: 9781919483283

10 9 8 7 6 5 4 3 2 1

Further copies of this publication can be purchased from www.salamanderstreet.com

"A tight, well-written and well-executed examination of a wider, recognisable societal problem—an England where there's always an excuse to have a drink, and seemingly no good reason to stop. Mature, intelligent work with plenty to say and a big heart."

Vicky Anderson—Made Up Liverpool

"Buckled is a brilliant new piece of writing from Helen Jeffery, sensitively exploring an important topic. Moving, humorous and excellently staged."

Elinor Randle—Artistic Director, Unity Theatre

"A 60-minute rollercoaster of a series of linear scenelets in the lives of Callum, a 30-something history teacher, his recovering alcoholic mother, and his childhood best friend, good-time girl, Ruby. The dialogue mixes some highly comedic moments with moments of real tenderness, and the further into the play you go the more emotionally charged it becomes. The end of the play offers hope, but does not give closure."

Number 9 Reviews

"Slick and thought-provoking, this show is packed with humanity and fits its one-hour format just right, leaving us with glimmers of hope for our characters' futures. It commendably avoids turning preachy and instead leaves us to make our own minds up as to where our own limits are, whilst giving a stark reminder of the consequences of going too far."

North West End Reviews

ACKNOWLEDGEMENTS

Thank you to Unity Theatre who commissioned the play as part of Up Next Festival 2023 and to Artistic Director Eli Randle for her ongoing support in the subsequent development of the production. Thanks also to Lane Paul Stewart for his support during the first shows at Shakespeare North Playhouse Studio.

Much gratitude to Sarah Drage, who openly shared her experiences with me during the initial writing and research stage. Also grateful to Anna Donaghey @thebigdrinkrethink for sponsoring the production/tour and for inviting me onto her podcast to talk about the show, as well as Clare Pooley, author of *The Sober Diaries* (featured in the play!)

Love and thanks to Gillian Hardie, Roxanne Male and David Rimmer for being part of the initial R&D and work-in-progress sharing at Liverpool Fringe. Gratitude also to Gill for her help in casting the 2025 tour where Tracy Spencer, Megan Cerys-Holland and Al Bollands played the roles of Maggie, Ruby and Callum.

Thank you to everyone who came to see the shows during the 2024 and 2025 tours—special shout out to the North West Sober Butterfly crew!

Thank you to Steven for his support in helping me turn the idea for this play into a reality—and to my best friends Marnie and Ali, who always support me in everything I do. Finally, thank you to my family—especially my Mum for always being there, and my children. You will always be my greatest achievement.

This play is dedicated to Alan Male.

Helen Jeffery
2026

Buckled was first performed 21-23 March 2024 at Shakespeare North Playhouse Studio with the following cast and creative team:

Maggie	**Helen Jeffery**
Callum	**David Rimmer**
Ruby	**Samantha Alton**

Writer & Director	**Helen Jeffery**
Movement Director	**Grace Goulding**
Dramaturgical Support	**Steven Horay**
Technical Support	**Team at Shakespeare North Playhouse**

With support from Unity Theatre Liverpool & Shakespeare North Playhouse

PRODUCTION NOTES

I wrote *Buckled* with an energetic performance style in mind. Fast, clean and rhythmic scene-changes form part of the action, alongside more naturalistic social observations from the characters regarding their relationship to alcohol and each other. The play requires physically versatile actors and begins/ends with a piece of spoken word called 'The Niggle.' This non-naturalistic style of performance is seen at other moments in the play—during Scene 4, when the actors transform into various characters 'in the pub' and during Scene 12, where we think we are watching Ruby's audition for *The Wizard of Oz*, before discovering it is a dream/nightmare.

In terms of staging, *Buckled* can be performed very simply so it is ideal for small spaces and student productions. Folding chairs and a small table can be used effectively and moved by the actors to represent various locations, along with key props e.g., bottles, a framed photo of Callum/Ceri, Maggie's 'letter of amends' and Ruby's 'duvet of doom' in the final scene.

Music can also play an important part in building pace/rhythm as well as showing shifts in mood. In our original production, we also used projections to highlight the number of days Maggie was sober as the action progressed e.g., 183 days. None of the above is set in stone and the piece can be adapted to suit your needs—enjoy!

TRIGGER WARNING

Alcohol dependency.

SUGGESTED AGE RANGE

14+

CREATIVE TEAM

Helen Jeffery | Writer & Performer: MAGGIE

Helen is a playwright, poet, performer and director. A graduate of the Liverpool Everyman Playwright's Programme she has had several plays produced including *The Brink* and *Gun Metal Blue*, a recipient of the Blink Theatre Award for new writing. Helen was commissioned by Unity Theatre, Liverpool to create *Buckled* as part of Up Next Festival 2023 and is delighted that, since then, it has toured to several venues in the North West. Helen is currently involved in developing a new play for stage, as well as working as a dramaturg through her company 'Sober Scribbles.' More information about this and her other projects can be found at linktr.ee/HelenJeffery.

David Rimmer | CALLUM

David was involved in *Buckled* from its first script-in-hand performance at the Liverpool Fringe Festival. Trained at Bristol Old Vic Theatre School and Trinity Laban Conservatoire of Music and Dance. Credits include: Dandini in *Cinderella* (Bradford Playhouse), Will in *Requires Improvement* (Evening Cat Productions), Sam in *Mrs Smith* (Kings Arms).

Samantha Alton | RUBY

Samantha has been acting professionally for well over a decade and continues to build an admirable, multifaceted portfolio. She recently played leading lady 'Annie' alongside Ricky Tomlinson in a nationwide tour of the musical comedy *Irish Annies* written by Asa Murphy *(2025*). Amongst many projects, some of her recent notable credits include; playing Nessa in *Desperate Scousewives* by Lynne Fitzgerald (2024-2026) and Fiona Forrester with other multi-role performances in *By the Waters of Liverpool* (UK Tour 2023). She also starred as Kitty Wilkinson in the one-woman spectacular *Kitty, Queen of the Washhouse* by Arts Groupie CIC (*2018-2024).*

Grace Goulding | Movement Director

Grace is an award-winning Welsh creator, Movement Director and Choreographer based in Liverpool, making high quality and ambitious work across dance, theatre, education and outreach since 2010. Through focused and playful spaces, she guides performers to explore in brave, empowering and joyously inclusive environments. She is passionate about telling honest stories in big-hearted and bold ways across a vast cross section of the arts and entertainment industries. Working nationally and internationally with artists and organisations including New Adventures, Rambert, Barefeet Theatre Zambia, The Met Gala with SHOWstudio, The European Opera Centre, The National Youth Arts of Wales, Alder Hey Children's Hospital, LIPA and several major theatres across Merseyside with longstanding relationships at Liverpool's, Unity, Empire and Everyman & Playhouse Theatres.

Steven Horay | Dramaturgical Support

Steven is a graduate of 'Creative Writing and Film Studies' from Liverpool John Moores University and a literary fiction/script writer and editor. Thematically, his work explores family dynamics, class, identity, addiction, mental health and societal structures. Steven is represented by Clare Coombes from The Liverpool Literary Agency and his first full length stage play *Saint Jason*, was performed as part of Up Next Festival at Unity Theatre, Liverpool in March 2026.

Helen Jeffery

Buckled

CHARACTERS

RUBY, 30

CALLUM, 31

MAGGIE, 52

NOTES ON THE PLAYSCRIPT

Parts in bold in Scene 1 and 4 are spoken in unison by the three actors.

SCENE 1: THE NIGGLE (PART ONE)

CALLUM: You tell yourself it's "**not a problem**"

RUBY: You don't have "**an issue**"

MAGGIE: You could stop any time you wanted **but you don't**

RUBY: You don't stop

MAGGIE: You keep going

ALL: **You go at every opportunity there is**

MAGGIE: It's your birthday

CALLUM: Her Birthday

RUBY: His birthday

CALLUM: It's the wedding

MAGGIE: The Christening

CALLUM: The Funeral

ALL: **It's the weekend**

CALLUM: The picnic

MAGGIE: The barbeque

RUBY: Friday

CALLUM: Saturday

MAGGIE: Sunday

CALLUM: It's a bad day

MAGGIE: Bad week

RUBY: Bad month

CALLUM: You deserve it

MAGGIE: It's a treat

RUBY: It's sociable

CALLUM: But sometimes there's no-one else there

RUBY: So what is it then?

Beat.

MAGGIE: Well, then it's a way to

RUBY: Take the edge off

MAGGIE: Blur the problems

CALLUM: Forget the stresses

RUBY: Work

MAGGIE: Kids

CALLUM: Life

RUBY: And you know what? "**It's fine**" abso -bloody-lutely " fine"

MAGGIE: Because you don't have a problem

RUBY: You could stop whenever you wanted

CALLUM: It's just that—you don't want to stop

RUBY: You don't want to stop

MAGGIE: You don't want to stop

ALL: **Not yet**

SCENE 2: PUB. FRIDAY NIGHT.

RUBY and CALLUM enter, greet each other and sit down.

RUBY: Cheers.

They clink drinks.

How long now till the big day?

CALLUM: 43 days.

RUBY: And you know that because..?

CALLUM: We've got a massive countdown calendar in the kitchen!

RUBY: Guest list shaping up?

CALLUM: Yeah, pretty good though we're paying for most of it ourselves so we're gonna have to be really strict on numbers. We're keeping the actual wedding to family and/

RUBY: /You inviting anyone from school?

CALLUM: Megan and Dan, Ritchie... Vicky, though I doubt she'll come as her due date's around then.

RUBY: Vicky's pregnant? Wow—I did NOT see that one coming. What happened to her and Sam travelling the world and living like hippies?

CALLUM: I guess they grew up. We've all got to sometimes and if you find the right person…

RUBY: *(unconvinced)* Mmmm.

CALLUM: How's it going with your new fella anyway?

RUBY: Good thanks.

CALLUM: Yeah?

RUBY: You don't need to sound so surprised!

CALLUM: I'm just happy for you—what's his name again?

RUBY: Matt.

RUBY drains the last of her drink

RUBY: Right. Same again?

CALLUM: Bloody hell you drank that quick.

RUBY: Friday night—got to make the most of it.

CALLUM: Aaah… go on then, but just a coke for me.

RUBY: Lightweight.

MAGGIE enters—speaks to the audience as if she is in an AA meeting .

175 DAYS

MAGGIE: Hello everyone. I'm Maggie and I... I've come tonight as I could do with some moral support. I'm meeting up with my son, Callum, after I leave here and, as some of you know, we've not been in contact this year—because of my drinking. Anyway, it's his birthday next week so I texted, said I'd really like to give him his card in person— and he agreed. I haven't felt this nervous since my Maths O level exam!

I've put some money in his card. 30 quid. It was really hard to find one without a reference to drink on. The ones in the shop were all 'bottoms up' and 'let the fun be-GIN.' In the end, I went for one with a picture of a puppy on the front. Callum always wanted a dog when he was growing up…

Tonight's the first time I'm going somewhere that serves alcohol since I stopped drinking. I try to avoid pubs for obvious reasons… Mind you, even my corner shop's got a bigger selection of booze than it does fruit and veg! Is yours the same? It's mad, isn't it? Anyway that's all I want to say tonight. I'll report back next time—give you all something to look forward to.

MAGGIE exits as the scene switches back to the pub.

RUBY enters with two more bottles. She drinks throughout the scene, in contrast to Callum, who barely touches his drink.

CALLUM: I said a coke!

RUBY: Oops. Did Ceri tell you I'd messaged her some suggestions for the hen do?

CALLUM: Yeah, she did—but the thing is, her mate's already sorted everything—

RUBY: Have they booked a package? Cos there's some great deals out there—/

CALLUM: /Ceri's not much of a drinker, so/

RUBY: / Palma, Malaga/

CALLUM: /they've planned something a bit more low key—

RUBY: /although Newcastle's pretty good too—I've had some cracking nights out there/

CALLUM: Ruby!

RUBY: What?

CALLUM: You're not listening to me.

RUBY: Eh?

CALLUM: Ceri's not doing any of that typical hen night stuff.

RUBY: What do you mean?

CALLUM: Blow up cocks, strippers, jelly shots. It's just not her thing.

RUBY: But it's her hen do!!

CALLUM: Yeah, but... well, her mates booked dinner, then a show at the theatre.

RUBY: The theatre? Are you serious? Jesus, how boring does she want to make it?

CALLUM: Look, if you must know, it was me who suggested Ceri invite you in the first place. I mean, let's be honest, you're *my* mate really, not hers.

RUBY: Oh, I see.

CALLUM: Sorry, I didn't mean/

RUBY: /No, no, it's fine… I'm not sure I wanna go now anyway... Hey, maybe I could come on your stag do?

CALLUM: Absolutely no chance.

RUBY: Awww c'mon... like you said, I'm YOUR friend really. Surely almost 20 years of friendship counts for something?

CALLUM: Ruby, you are NOT coming on my stag do, so you might as well save your breath!

RUBY: Spoilsport. What have you got planned anyway? Visit to a museum? Trip to the library?

CALLUM: I'm not sure yet. Probably just go for a Chinese or something.

RUBY: A Chinese? For your Stag Do? Jesus. What has she done to you?

CALLUM: *(glancing at his watch)* Listen, I'm gonna have to shoot—I'm off to meet my Mum.

RUBY: Have you patched things up then?

CALLUM: Not really. It's just she messaged me last week—said she wanted to see me and—what with the wedding and everything... Ceri thinks I'll regret it later, if she's not there.

RUBY: I've always liked your Mum. She was such a laugh when we were growing up. Hey, do you remember your birthday when she came in with the karaoke machine from the pub? It was so funny and... *(she stops when she sees his face.)*

CALLUM: *(Looking at his watch again)* Listen, I've gotta go or she'll be half-cut by the time I get there. Speak to you soon, yeah?

RUBY: Course. Say hi to your Mum from me... *(as an afterthought)* and Ceri...

SCENE 3: RESTAURANT.
175 DAYS

MAGGIE sits at a table with a coke and a bottle of Peroni in front of her. She unzips her handbag and retrieves a mirror—checks her reflection—puts it back in her bag. She looks at her watch. Picks up a menu.

CALLUM enters. He spots MAGGIE before she sees him and takes a deep breath.

MAGGIE: *(looking up and smiling)* Hello, love.

She stands up to hug him but he takes a step back.

MAGGIE sits back down.

I got you a drink. Peroni. I think that's what you like.

He nods and sits down awkwardly opposite MAGGIE.

MAGGIE: So... how are you?

CALLUM: Fine.

MAGGIE: How's Ceri?

CALLUM: She's fine too.

He takes a drink.

MAGGIE: Still doing her yoga?

CALLUM: Pilates.

MAGGIE: Pilates, that's right.

Pause.

MAGGIE: Your friend okay?

CALLUM: Sorry?

MAGGIE: You said you were meeting a friend—before coming here?

CALLUM: Oh, yeah.

MAGGIE: Anyone I know?

CALLUM: Ruby.

MAGGIE: Aww… how is she? I haven't seen her for ages!

CALLUM: She's… Ruby.

MAGGIE smiles.

MAGGIE: You're looking well. Being engaged suits you.

CALLUM: Does it?

MAGGIE: *(Nodding to the menu)* They do a lovely carbonara in here.

CALLUM: It's a bit heavy.

MAGGIE: Or pizza? You love pizza don't you?

CALLUM: Mum, I haven't even looked at the menu yet!

She passes him the menu.

CALLUM: This is the cocktail menu.

MAGGIE: Other side.

CALLUM: *(He studies it for a second then nods towards her drink)* What are you on—vodka and coke?

MAGGIE: Just a coke.

CALLUM snorts.

MAGGIE: What?

CALLUM: Is that meant to impress me?

MAGGIE: No.

Pause.

MAGGIE: I—I—was really pleased you agreed to see me tonight, love.

CALLUM: Mmmm.

MAGGIE: I can't believe that you're 31 next week, I—

CALLUM: /Listen, Mum, I'm only here because of Ceri. You know what she's like—always wants to fix things... and what with the wedding coming up...

MAGGIE: How's it going—are you on top of everything?

CALLUM: Pretty much—we've booked the venue, sorted the cars. Just got to finalise the guest list.

MAGGIE: *(teasing)* Will I be getting an invite then?

CALLUM looks hard at MAGGIE.

MAGGIE: Sorry.

Pause.

How's everything at school?

CALLUM: It's fine. *Now.*

Beat.

MAGGIE: That's good. Makes me feel a bit better.

CALLUM: *(stiffly)* How have you been?

MAGGIE: Up and down.

Callum waits for her

MAGGIE: You see, the thing is—when you stopped answering my calls—and messages— I knew I had to…

CALLUM: Sort your shit out?

MAGGIE: Do something.

He waits.

MAGGIE: About my drinking

CALLUM: And? Have you?

MAGGIE: Yes.

Pause.

CALLUM: You've actually stopped drinking?

MAGGIE: I have.

CALLUM: For how long this time? A day? A week?

MAGGIE: Almost six months. I've been going to meetings. Doing it properly.

CALLUM digests this.

CALLUM: Sorry I... I mean obviously I'm glad you've stopped... but, well, we've been here before haven't we—what's different this time?

MAGGIE: This time I know how important it is. I—I don't want to let you down—or Ceri.

CALLUM: It's a shame you didn't feel like that when I was growing up.

MAGGIE: Callum!

CALLUM: *(Frustrated)* I'm sorry, Mum, but do you not remember all those time I asked you, begged you, to stop drinking when I was a kid/

MAGGIE: That's not fair—I did stop—

CALLUM: /Yeah you did—for a week or two—and then you'd start again. Make out like it was no big deal—that I was just being dramatic. That everyone drank.

MAGGIE: Times were different back then.

CALLUM: That's bullshit! No one else's Mum drank like you did.

MAGGIE: You're making me out to be some sort of monster!

CALLUM: And if I did try and talk to you about your drinking, you'd make it seem like I was the unreasonable one…

MAGGIE: You know what, I thought you'd be happy I've stopped drinking but it's never enough is it? I could turn up with a winning lottery ticket and you'd say I bought the wrong biscuits!

CALLUM starts to get up... putting on his coat.

Oh Callum, wait—sit down. We haven't even ordered yet!

CALLUM: I'm not hungry.

She rummages in her bag—finds the card and holds it out to him.

MAGGIE: Will you at least take this? It's—it's for your birthday.

CALLUM reluctantly accepts.

MAGGIE: Can I see you—next week I mean?

CALLUM: Ceri and I have already made plans.

MAGGIE: Course you have.

CALLUM: Listen... I'll give you a call yeah?

MAGGIE: Okay, love… look after yourself, won't you?

As CALLUM exits, MAGGIE sits and stares at the Peroni bottle for a very long time.

SCENE 4: RUBY'S FLAT.

RUBY is doing her makeup, dressing gown on, singing along to music.

RUBY: Saturday lunch time.

She drinks.

Don't judge—we've all been there—gone for a couple of pints that's turned into a sesh. I've always been pretty lucky—never really suffered from hangovers. Until I hit 30 *(she laughs)* not enough to make me pack up drinking though.

She drinks.

It's Megan's leaving-do tonight. Lucky bitch has managed to bag herself a six-month stint on a musical. Most of us that work in the call centre are actors—selling our souls whilst we wait for a break. It's hard to find a job that gives you time off for auditions but flexibility comes at a price—in this case, minimum wage. I'm not staying with the work lot all night though—I'm meeting Matt later, then tomorrow we're going to my sister's. It's her birthday so we're having this family lunch thing.

I'm definitely gonna need a few drinks to get through that.

She drinks

My sister, Laura, she's only two years older than me, but her life's so... so sorted. Married 'tick'. Own house and car 'tick'. Good job 'tick'. Plus now she's pregnant, everyone treats her like she's some sort of princess.

Urgh—I sound like a right bitch don't I?

She laughs

I never used to mind family get-togethers—when my Dad was around... and I do love them, my Mum and my sister, it's just, sometimes it's hard always being the one that's a disappointment.

Right, what time is it? Ooh better get my glad rags on!

Movement sequence with all the actors playing different characters in pub—sections in BOLD are spoken in unison—emphasis on the rhythm/rhyme at the end of lines.

MAGGIE: Weddings and birthdays, parties and catch ups

CALLUM: We soak up them all with a drink

RUBY: We've got bottomless brunches—happy hour cocktails

CALLUM: You'd be mad to refuse

MAGGIE: Don't you think?

RUBY: Whatever your bevvy/ there's endless promotions

CALLUM: Deals and those 2-for-1 offers

MAGGIE: Go on, '**get 'em down you**' /There's time for a swift one

RUBY: Let us help you empty your coffers

CALLUM: Cos from Monday to Sunday/ And sunrise to sunset

ALL: **There's always the time for a drink**

MAGGIE: If you can't hack the pace

CALLUM: Have a half, not a pint

RUBY: Raise your glass

ALL: **Get a smile on your face**

MAGGIE: So push down your worries

CALLUM: Ignore all your problems

RUBY: Sink your woes in the base of a jar

MAGGIE: Drink won't solve your trouble

RUBY: Unless it's a double

ALL: **So cheers! Now get to the bar**

SCENE 5: AA/SUPPORT GROUP. 176 DAYS

The two scenes take place simultaneously but in different locations. MAGGIE is at an AA meeting and CALLUM is in a support group for children of alcoholics

MAGGIE: Hello everyone. I'm Maggie and... I'm struggling. I—I almost drank last night—but I didn't.

CALLUM: Hi everyone. I'm Callum… it was my fiancée, Ceri's, idea that I come. I didn't even know that there were groups like this, for children of alcoholics, until she gave me the leaflet.

MAGGIE: I'm not sure what I thought would happen when I told my son I'd stopped drinking. Actually that's a lie—I had hoped he'd be pleased—but maybe after everything that's happened that was too much to expect?

CALLUM: She thinks it might help me to talk to other people about my Mum and, well, the impact her drinking has had on me. You see, until a couple of days ago, I hadn't seen her for a few months—not since my school production. I'm a history teacher but I was helping out with lighting and backstage.

Beat.

I don't usually talk about work with my Mum because, well, she doesn't remember stuff a lot of the time. Is that the same for any of you? But for some reason, I did mention the show to her. Big mistake.

MAGGIE: You see, he's a teacher, our Callum, and when he told me he'd been helping out with the school production I asked him about tickets to come and see it. That was when he went all quiet on me—said he didn't know if there were any left—which I thought was a bit weird. I mean surely he could ask them to put one aside for his Mum? In the end, I rang the school office and when they told me there were tickets on the door I thought —brilliant—I'll surprise him.

CALLUM: I couldn't believe it when she just turned up. I really didn't want her there. It sounds harsh but, well, she's got form for messing things up.

MAGGIE: Anyway I must have got the time wrong because, when I arrived, the show had already started. I could see there were still a few seats at the back though—

CALLUM: As soon as I saw her, I knew she'd been drinking.

MAGGIE: /so I thought I'd just make my way there. The only problem was it was quite dark, so I stumbled and lost my footing. You know what those halls are like—they polish the floors don't they?

CALLUM: She was stumbling everywhere, then she dropped her bag and everything fell out—including the empties she'd obviously drunk on the way. Can you imagine? I was absolutely mortified.

MAGGIE: It wasn't like they had to stop the show—well, only for a minute or two. One of the teachers, at least I think he was one of the teachers—helped me outside and Ceri, that's Callum's girlfriend, went and got me a chair to sit on while I waited for a taxi to arrive and take me home.

CALLUM: The *Head* took her outside. Oh, he was all smiles when he came back in but he was obviously pissed off. I could see him shaking his head and muttering to the Deputy. I went over to him in the interval—tried to apologise—but he just brushed me off…

MAGGIE: I had to wait ages for the taxi—in fact I was still there during the interval when Callum came outside—

CALLUM: It was so embarrassing and I was fuming she'd messed things up again.

MAGGIE: /I thought he'd come to see if I was okay but instead he had a go at me!! Told me he didn't want to see me again unless I stopped drinking.

CALLUM: So, yeah—in a nutshell—that's my relationship with my Mum.

He laughs

Can you see why I might need some support?

MAGGIE: At first I was fuming with him... then I was angry with myself... and now... well, here we are.

I haven't had a drink in 176 days—and at least he's talking to me again. That's got to be a good sign, hasn't it?

SCENE 6: RUBY'S FLAT.

Sunday Morning. RUBY creeps in slowly with a glass of water in hand. She is horribly hungover. A pair of men's boxers and a bra lie discarded on the floor.

RUBY sits on the sofa and takes a large gulp of water. She retches.

RUBY: *(Leaning forward, whispering)* There's a man in my bed.

Beat.

It's not Matt.

She takes another big gulp of water—visibly sweaty, anxious, jittery

I've no idea who he is or how he ended up back here. Everything is just blank. Complete nothingness.

She thinks

I remember going to Megan's leaving thing—there was a lot of Prosecco—and then someone suggested we go onto another bar.

Trying to piece it together.

There was definitely karaoke and then…

She stops—looks for her bag and retrieves her phone from it.

Shit. I've got loads of missed calls and messages. Two from Megan. Three from Matt.

Reading messages.

8:47: Matt: Hey Ruby. You left me a message but all I can hear is noise. Are you on your way?

8:53: Megan: I can't believe you did that tonight—it was my leaving do and you still had to make it all about you.

9:13: Matt: I've tried calling you back a few times but it just goes to voicemail. I'll give you another 10 mins then head home.

9:29: Megan: What you said about me and Neil was unforgivable. *(to herself) Shit! (continues reading)* I hope you get the help you need—you obviously have a problem!

12:33: Matt: ARE YOU OK?

RUBY: *(To herself)* No.

She stands up slowly making a feeble attempt to tidy up and tentatively picking up the man's trousers off the floor before retching.

Urgh.

MALE VOICE *(O/S)*: RUBY... Any chance of a coffee?

She stops.

RUBY: Oh God. *(Shouting)* Yep —be right with you.

Beat.

What is his name?

SCENE 7: MAGGIE AA MEETING.
178 DAYS

MAGGIE: Do you know what the hardest thing is about not drinking? Well, to be fair, you probably do... I think it's that, even when you stop—everyone else is still drinking. It's like being the only kid in the class that's not invited to the party! Then, when you tell people that you're not drinking, it's as if they're disappointed in you—or worried that you're going to turn into this big 'party pooper' who insists everyone drinks lemonade! The other thing I've noticed is that people start to justify their own drinking so they can reassure themselves that they're nothing like you. I'm like, 'listen, I don't care whether you drink every night or once a week—this isn't about you. If you haven't got a problem with your drinking then you crack on!'

When you don't—when you can't drink—well, it's bloody tough. Not so much physically cos I've passed the permanent headache stage now and look *(she holds out her hand)* no shaking. No, I'm talking about the social aspect of not drinking. Being the odd one out, because, well, booze—it binds everyone together, doesn't it? It doesn't matter what class you are, or how much money you've got, drinking is the party that everyone can join.

You know I thought giving up smoking was tough—but at least when I did that I got a pat on the back.

No one says 'well done' when you stop drinking, do they?

SCENE 8: PARK.

Monday 4.30pm - RUBY sits on a bench. CALLUM walks over with two coffees .

RUBY: Fancy seeing you here!

CALLUM: I know... and with two coffees too...

He scrutinizes the bench.

This is never 'our' bench?

RUBY: The very same.

CALLUM: God—the number of weekends we spent hanging out here as kids... Anyway listen, I can't stay long—got lessons to plan for tomorrow. Are you okay? You sounded awful on the phone.

RUBY: I feel crap.

CALLUM: You don't look great. Hangover?

RUBY: I think I've got a bug or something... er, listen Cal, I don't suppose you might be able to sub me til I get paid next week?

CALLUM: Ah Ruby... cash is really tight at the minute, what with the wedding and everything.

RUBY: Please Cal. I wouldn't ask if I wasn't desperate—and I can't ask my Mum—or Laura.

CALLUM: Why not?

RUBY: I'm in the dog house aren't I? I bailed out of her birthday lunch yesterday.

Beat.

Please.

CALLUM: How much do you need?

RUBY: A hundred? My agent called earlier—she's lined me up for a big audition on Thursday—but it's in London.

CALLUM: What's it for?

RUBY: A new version of ***The Wizard of Oz***. I sent a self tape in and now they want to see me. The only downside is I've got to get a really early train… and the tickets are expensive…

CALLUM: Okay—but this has got to be the last time.

He transfers the money on his phone

Sent it.

RUBY: Aw thanks, Cal. You're a star. Anyway enough about me—how was your Mum when you saw her—was she okay?

CALLUM: I guess so... claims she's stopped drinking.

RUBY: Really? For how long?

CALLUM: Nearly six months.

RUBY: Wow—hats off to her. I don't think I could do it...

CALLUM: Now there's a surprise.

RUBY: I couldn't even manage Dry January—and I mean, it's not like she needs to pack it in completely is it?

CALLUM: No?

RUBY: It's not like she's an alcoholic/

CALLUM: Right.

RUBY: /Necking cider out of a brown paper bag or having a drink as soon as she wakes up.

CALLUM: /I might have known you'd take her side.

RUBY: I didn't know there were any sides... God Cal, where's all this come from?

CALLUM: I just... I just wish she could have stopped when I was growing up. She's only stopped now because she wants an invite to the wedding—it won't last.

RUBY: I think you're being a bit dramatic Cal. Okay, your Mum's always liked a drink—but there's nothing wrong with that, is there?

CALLUM says nothing.

RUBY: Is it Ceri who's putting all these ideas in your head?

CALLUM: What?

RUBY: About your Mum—and me probably. Is that why she doesn't want me to go on her hen do?

CALLUM: You said you didn't want to go!

RUBY: It is, isn't it? She's worried I might pour alcohol down her throat and force her to have a good time!

CALLUM: Ruby, we're not kids anymore—why does everything have to revolve around drinking?

RUBY: Christ—she has got to you hasn't she?

CALLUM: I haven't got time for this.

RUBY: For what?

CALLUM stands up and starts to put his coat on.

Where are you going?

CALLUM: Home Ruby. I'm going home. I told you, I've got lessons to plan... I'll see you soon, yeah?

He exits.

RUBY: Jesus. Who pissed on his chips?

SCENE 9: AA/SUPPORT GROUP.
179 DAYS

The scenes take place simultaneously but in different locations. MAGGIE is at an AA meeting and CALLUM is in a support group for children of alcoholics.

MAGGIE: I—I've been thinking a lot about the past recently; that's the thing about being sober—you suddenly have all these extra hours in the day. In some ways it's good—the house has never been so tidy—but it also means I've had a lot of time to think about the past—the things that I did. Things I didn't…

CALLUM: Drinking in our house when I was growing up... well, it was just the norm. I remember when I was at uni, telling a friend about us leaving whisky for Santa on Christmas Eve and he was like—"You what? On what planet would Santa ever be able to ride his sleigh half cut?"

MAGGIE: I was so young when I fell pregnant with Callum, barely out of my teens—terrified of what my parents would say. In the end I only told my Mum—asked her to tell my Dad. I'll never forget the look on his face after she had.

Beat.

Of course, being the only one of my friends with a baby was a novelty at first—everyone popping over, bringing pressies and wanting a cuddle. Didn't last though. Who wants to listen to a baby screaming when you could be out having fun? I found out they'd all been on a 'girls' holiday' to Corfu without telling me and that was when I realised. This was my life now—22 and a single mum.

CALLUM: I don't want to paint my Mum as some sort of villain though, cos I do have good memories. Trips to the park—swimming—even just curling up on the sofa and watching films together. When she wasn't drinking, things were very different/

MAGGIE: /My Mum did what she could to help me, but it wasn't the same as having a partner. I did try and reach out to Callum's Dad a couple of times but he wasn't interested. He had his own life to get on with and he made that clear.

CALLUM: /and of course she was bringing me up on her own *(as if to someone in the group)* My Dad? I don't know—I never saw him—but my Mum just clammed up if I asked her about him. My Nan wouldn't tell me anything either—said it was probably best if I just let 'sleeping dogs lie'... whatever the hell that meant.

MAGGIE: When Callum started school, I decided to get myself a job. It wasn't easy finding something to fit in around him but I managed to get some lunchtime shifts in a local pub. Then as he got older, I worked evenings too. There'd always be a few drinks at the end of a shift and, sometimes, we'd have lock-ins. Billy, that's the landlord, he'd get me on the karaoke—I loved to sing! Between us, I think he had a bit of a crush on me…

CALLUM: You know last week, when we were talking about significant moments? Well I've remembered something that happened on my 12th birthday. I don't think I've even told Ceri about this/

MAGGIE: By the time Callum was at secondary school I was drinking every day. I knew, deep down, that it was bad for me, but I didn't stop. I tried from time to time... but I never managed more than a couple of weeks.

CALLUM: My Mum said I could have some mates over—that we could watch a film and she'd pop to the shop to get some pizzas and party food. I was dead excited because my mate, Ruby, said she'd bring her mate, Stacey, and I really fancied her. Anyway, we were all in the living room watching ***Pirates of the Caribbean Dead Man's Chest*** and getting hungry. There was no sign of my Mum so I tried phoning her but it just went to voicemail. In the end I rang my Nan and luckily she answered and came straight over with a load of fish and chips for us all. We were just finishing the food when my Mum came home. I could smell her before I could see her—stinking of booze and fags. She stumbled in with this karaoke machine she'd 'borrowed' from a fella at the pub and was hell-bent on plugging it in and getting everyone to sing. I was so embarrassed—and so was Stacey, who suddenly remembered she had to 'help her Mum with something' and practically ran out the door.

After everyone left, my Mum gave me this crumpled looking card. It said 'Hope you have an amazing day.' I threw it straight in the bin and went to my Nan's for the night.

MAGGIE: The thing is, by then, I wasn't even getting any pleasure from drinking—it was more I felt anxious if I couldn't have a drink. I'd often have the shakes of a morning and the only thing that helped was to have another drink.

CALLUM: I don't know why I ever thought having my mates round was a good idea. I never invited anyone again, well, except for Ruby. Kids at school were brutal—it was all "my Dad says your Mum's a pisshead", "my sister saw your Mum in a right mess"—stuff like that. I tried to laugh it off but inside I was... ashamed.

MAGGIE: I don't think anyone around me really knew how much I was putting away—I was pretty crafty at hiding bottles or burying them at the bottom of the bins. By this time, drinking was all that mattered. It made everything more bearable, took the edge off reality and helped to numb my emotions.

CALLUM: You know, at some sort of subconscious level, I think I blamed myself for my Mum's drinking. Was I not enough? Why did she have to drink all the time? I remember I used to go looking for bottles she'd hidden, empty them down the sink and then smash them to pieces outside in the yard. Just for a few minutes that made me feel better.

MAGGIE: And now? Well, those feelings have all come back, haven't they? I've pushed them down for 30 years and suddenly, with no booze to hide behind, they've found a way to rise to the surface and I'm drowning in shame and regret. That's what I feel more than anything. Ashamed. I wish I could put it right. Go back and do it all again without a drink in my hand. But I can't, can I?

CALLUM: Ceri says I need time to process everything that happened when I was growing up—to try to understand why my Mum drank the way she did, but at the moment, all I can think about is the wedding and whether we should invite her. What do you think?

SCENE 10: RUBY'S FLAT.

Lights up on RUBY script in her hand, rehearsing lines.

RUBY: I lost my job yesterday.

I knew it was on the cards after I rang in sick again so, it wasn't a surprise when 'Neil' called me into his office.

Ruby becomes 'Neil'.

NEIL: Sit down, Ruby.

RUBY: What's this about, Neil?

NEIL: Well, you see the thing is, Ruby, myself and Carol [she's a right bitch] just wanted to check in with you—make sure everything's okay?

RUBY: Yeah, everything's fine thanks. Why?

NEIL: It's just you've taken quite a bit of time off this year and there does seem to be a pattern with your absences, Ruby.

RUBY: A pattern?

NEIL: Yes, Carol and I have noticed that it's mostly Monday mornings that you ring in sick and, to be honest, we were a little alarmed by your behaviour at Megan's leaving do on Saturday.

RUBY: Anyway, I'm not gonna bore you with the rest of it but suffice to say, Neil and I have now parted company.

It's a blessing really, 'cos now I've got the chance to learn my lines and rehearse for my audition in Manchester tomorrow.

Right, c'mon, Ruby. Focus.

She holds out her hand—it shakes.

I don't know why I'm so nervous. I haven't felt like this since Bella and I auditioned for Lady Macbeth at Drama School. She got it.

She drinks.

I've not heard from Callum either. I thought he might have texted by now but nothing. Don't know why I'm surprised—things between us haven't been the same since he started going out with Ceri. I've never taken to her—for a start she hardly drinks and her idea of a good time is going to pilates. Oh, and she's a vegan.

You know who I feel really sorry for though? Callum's Mum — Maggie. I mean saying she's an alcoholic—it's a bit extreme — and anyway, if she was, then surely she deserves to be supported, not ignored. I might go round to her house later, see if she's okay? We always got on well when I was younger.

Her phone bleeps—she picks it up.

Matt.

She turns it upside down.

I'd better read this—I've been a bit off with him lately, you know, after what happened?

She reads.

I don't believe this—He's only gone and bloody dumped me! Listen to this: "I don't think we have the same outlook on life and I'd prefer to be with someone whose main priority isn't drinking."

Who does the fuck does he think he is?

She reaches forward, grabs the wine bottle and tops up her glass.

Sanctimonious twat!

SCENE 11: AA MEETING.
180 DAYS

MAGGIE: I've taken a big step this week and I've written a letter to my son, Callum. Someone in a previous meeting called it "making amends"—which is a good way of putting it. I don't know whether I'm gonna send it yet—or even if I should? You see, I'm reading this book at the minute and in it, the writer talks about recognising that even though you might feel you need to apologise for things you've done, sometimes, it's kinder—for the person you've written to—not to send it. Am I making sense? Anyway for now, I'll just keep it in my handbag—until I'm sure.

So, apart from writing to Callum, this week I've been thinking a lot about who first decided we had to drink to have a good time. I mean, seriously I'd like to have words with that person! Cos' there's definitely an expectation isn't there? Start drinking in your teens, get hammered on your 18th and then basically keep going.

(Quickly) I'm not judging anyone who drinks by the way. I mean how can I? The truth of it is, I wish I still could. My God, I'm jealous of people who can manage their drinking—just have one or two on a special occasion—cos I know that's not me.

Pause.

I do sometimes wonder if I might, one day, be able to drink normally again? I even thought about trying one of those non-alcoholic beers last weekend but I wasn't sure if that was a good idea?

(as if to someone in the meeting) What's that? Non-alcoholic beers are for non-alcoholics?

Alcoholic. I'm not sure how I feel about using that term—not to describe myself anyway. It just sounds so... severe...

I guess I'm just thinking about things in a different way now. I mean I always thought people who liked a drink were a laugh, fun and that people who didn't drink were boring. Even when I worked in the pub, if someone ordered a soft drink I'd be like "Oh go on, have a proper drink. Just have one."

God. Maybe I was part of the problem?

SCENE 12: 'DREAM SEQUENCE'.

RUBY's audition for 'The Wizard of Oz.' It is the perfect audition… which comes to an end as we hear the sound of a mobile phone ringing.

RUBY: *(reaching for her mobile)* Urgghhh…hello?

Hold on, it's… shit shit shit shit shit.

Fuck—I must have slept through my alarm.

Can you ring them back? See if they'll see me this afternoon?

Look, I'm really sorry—I just… I just…

Yeah, it's okay.

No, I understand.

Sorry.

I'm really sorry.

She looks at her phone for a long time before hurling it across the room in a fit of frustration as she screams 'arrghhhhh'.

SCENE 13: CALLUM'S FLAT.
182 DAYS

CALLUM opens the letter from MAGGIE and reads:

CALLUM: Dear Callum—I'm sorry it's taken me until now to write this letter. I should have done it sooner but I guess I wasn't really ready then. I've been thinking a lot about the impact my drinking must have had on you when you were growing up and, well, I'm really ashamed.

MAGGIE enters—she reads sections of the letter.

CALLUM: I want to apologise for some of the things I did and I really hope that in doing so, I won't upset you more than I already have.

He takes a deep breath.

I'm sorry for not being the Mum that you deserved.

MAGGIE: For the times I didn't make you breakfast, walk you to school or pick you up. I'm sorry for planning days out that involved a trip to the pub or ways for me to drink. For embarrassing you when your mates came over. For ruining your 12th birthday and for turning up drunk at your Parents Evening and kicking off at your teacher.

CALLUM: *(aside)* To be fair I didn't mind that—Mr Higgs was a right tosser.

MAGGIE: I'm sorry for all those times that you had to pick me up off the floor and put me to bed. I'm sorry you had to see me covered in sick—and worse—and I'm sorry that you were the one that had to clean me up. I'm sorry for the times that you slept on the floor next to me.

CALLUM: *(Aside)* I always worried she might choke.

MAGGIE: I'm sorry you had to look after me. That was wrong love—it was *my* responsibility to look after you and I messed up so many times.

CALLUM: I only thank God that your Nan was there to pick up the pieces. I miss her a lot and I know you do too—perhaps we can talk about this one day?

MAGGIE: I'm sorry I got drunk on the day of your school show and I'm sorry for not telling you every single day...

CALLUM: ...how proud of you I am.

MAGGIE: Proud of the man you've become—*in spite of*, not because of me.

CALLUM: Proud that you've got yourself sorted. That you have a good job, your own home, someone you love. Finally...

MAGGIE: ...although there are probably countless other times that you remember and I do not...

CALLUM: ...I am sorry that I won't be at your wedding...

MAGGIE: ...and I understand why you can't invite me.

MAGGIE exits.

CALLUM: I hope you both have the wonderful day that you deserve.

Thank you for reading this. Lots of love Mum x

CALLUM folds up the letter. He doesn't speak but is visibly moved.

SCENE 14: THE PARK. SATURDAY MORNING. 183 DAYS

MAGGIE is sat on a bench reading 'The Sober Diaries' when CALLUM appears.

CALLUM: Hiya, Mum.

MAGGIE: *(looks up)* Hi love.

CALLUM: *(indicating the book)* Any good?

MAGGIE: Yeah—it's not bad actually.

They sit silent for a moment and then both speak simultaneously.

CALLUM: Look, Mum/

MAGGIE: /Listen, love.

CALLUM: Go on, you first.

MAGGIE: You read my letter then?

CALLUM: I did.

They just look at each other.

CALLUM: I just want to say… well, I want to say thank you for writing it. It can't have been easy.

MAGGIE: It wasn't. But the funny thing is, once I'd posted it, I did feel better. Lighter. *(Quickly)* It wasn't just a way for me to unburden myself and lay everything at your door though... whether you choose to forgive me, well, that's up to you.

CALLUM: I want to forgive you, Mum, but first I need to be able to trust you. When you were drinking I couldn't do that. I never knew which version of you I was going to get.

MAGGIE: I'm so sorry—if I could just/

CALLUM: /I don't want you to keep saying sorry. What's done is done. It's just, I've wanted you to stop drinking for so long and, well, now that you have, I'm just not sure I believe it.

MAGGIE: I'm not sure I believe it myself love but, as of today, I am officially 183 days sober.

CALLUM: Not that you're counting?

MAGGIE: Oh, I am. Every single bloody day!

CALLUM: And how does it feel to be... 183 days sober?

MAGGIE: Terrifying. But also good... It's not like I've started surfing this pink cloud that the celebrities talk about, but I am sleeping better. I don't feel as anxious, and—did I tell you that I've got myself a job? Just part time—in a cafe—I start next week.

CALLUM: That's great.

MAGGIE: Yeah. It kind of is... and the best thing is that no-one there knows me as a drinker.

CALLUM: Wow.

MAGGIE: I know. When I went in last week to sort out my shifts, it was someone's birthday so the boss bought a cake and some fizz. When they offered me a glass, and I said I didn't drink, no one even batted an eyelid. Can you imagine... me turning down some free fizz?

CALLUM smiles.

CALLUM: And what would you do, say, if you were at a wedding —and someone offered you a drink?

MAGGIE: I'd just say no thank you.

CALLUM: And what if they asked you why you weren't drinking?

MAGGIE: I'd tell them.

CALLUM: Tell them what?

MAGGIE: Tell them that, for me, alcohol isn't an option—and hope that they'd leave it at that.

CALLUM: And if they didn't?

MAGGIE: Then I'd tell them to fuck off and mind their own business!

CALLUM laughs

CALLUM: Cos, the thing is Mum—we do want to invite you to the wedding. It's just that there's gonna be a lot of people there drinking and some of them wondering why you're not. Do you think you can handle that? Because if you can't, I need you to be honest with me.

MAGGIE takes CALLUM's hands in hers and looks him straight in the eye.

MAGGIE: I want to see you get married more than anything in the world so—if it's alright with you and Ceri—I'd like to come to the ceremony, be in the photos and everything and then... just play it by ear. I'm not sure I can manage the whole day but if I know I can leave, if or when I need to, then I think that could work. Would that be okay with you?

CALLUM: Yeah. I think that would be okay with me.

He reaches into his pocket, takes out the invitation and hands it to her. They hug.

SCENE 15: CALLUM AND CERI'S FLAT.

RUBY enters. She has obviously been drinking.

RUBY: What the hell is this? The evening do? We've been friends for almost 20 years and you invite me to the evening do?

CALLUM: Listen, I didn't want to just post it—I wanted to explain—but I tried calling and your phone just kept—

RUBY: /Yeah it's broken *(laughs)* like us, by the look of things. So, come on—let's hear it? Why haven't I been invited to the actual wedding?

CALLUM: Will you sit down? Can we talk about this?

RUBY: It's Ceri isn't it? She's never liked me.

CALLUM: I did try and explain to you a while back that we were having to be strict with numbers on the day itself—

RUBY: I didn't realise I was a number—I thought we were mates?

Pause.

RUBY: Wow o-kay, I see. Jeez nice to know when you're valued isn't it?

(Looking around) Have you got anything to drink?

CALLUM: I don't think that's a good idea—it's barely 5 o'clock—you've obviously already had a few.

RUBY: Oh fuck off, Callum! What are you—a Saint or something?

CALLUM: Ruby, just calm down.

RUBY: I've got it, yeah, yeah you'll like this one... Arise, Sir Callum—patron saint of pissheads!

CALLUM: Look, I'm sorry that we can only invite you to the evening do—but/

RUBY: /But what?

CALLUM: Well, if you feel that angry about it, then maybe it's better you don't come at all.

RUBY: Are you being serious?

CALLUM: I don't want to be worrying that you're going to cause a scene, or get drunk and—

RUBY: What—enjoy myself? Have fun? You've obviously forgotten what that looks like cos since you've been with Ceri you've turned into a right boring bastard.

CALLUM: I want you to leave. This isn't helping either of us.

RUBY: Has Ceri put you up to this?

CALLUM: This has nothing to do with Ceri!

RUBY: She's always been jealous, jealous of me.

CALLUM: You know you've got a problem—with your drinking—don't you? And you need to sort it out now Ruby, before everything turns to shit. I've been here before—and you know, after everything I've been through with my Mum—

RUBY: *(mimicking)* Your Mum, your Mum. You know what? I feel sorry for your Mum! No wonder she drank as much as she did. You probably drove her to drink with your bloody moaning and whining and/

CALLUM points to the door.

CALLUM: I want you to leave. NOW!

RUBY: Fine, I'm going and you know where you can stick your invite to the evening do!

SCENE 16: RUBY'S FLAT. 189 DAYS

RUBY's Flat—the place is a mess, bottles everywhere. RUBY is passed out on the sofa covered in a duvet that has seen better days.

MAGGIE knocks repeatedly before realising the door is open.

MAGGIE: Ruby? Ruby, are you here?

Spotting RUBY on the sofa she moves over to her.

Oh my God! Ruby—are you okay?

RUBY: Maggie? What are you doing here?

MAGGIE: Callum asked me to return your spare key. The one you gave him when you kept locking yourself out? I didn't need to use it though—you know your door was open?

RUBY: Aaaaah… well, as you can see—I am most definitely in.

She laughs

You wanna drink?

MAGGIE: No.

RUBY: Oops sorry—I forgot. You're on the wagon aren't you? Well, shhh, I won't tell anyone if you don't...

MAGGIE: I wouldn't mind a cup of tea. I can make it if you like?

RUBY: Haven't got any milk in... and anyway it's Saturday night… have a drink with me.

MAGGIE: Or coffee? I could make us a black coffee?

RUBY: Ohhhh Maggie—don't be so BOR-ING.

MAGGIE: Have you got any bin bags? I'll give you a hand to clear up.

She exits to kitchen.

RUBY: Why should I care? I'm moving out anyway.

MAGGIE: Are you?

RUBY: Yeah, the landlord did an inspection and he's given me my marching orders.

MAGGIE: *(re-entering)* So, what will you do?

RUBY: Dunno.

MAGGIE: Will you move back to your Mum's?

RUBY: Urrgh… God, no. She wouldn't want me anyway. She's too preoccupied with my sister and getting ready to be a Grandma.

MAGGIE: Aww… that's nice. So you're going to be an Aunty then?

RUBY: Never had you down as the maternal type, Maggie…

MAGGIE: I wish I had been.

RUBY: You don't.

Beat.

MAGGIE: She tried to talk to me once you know, your Mum? At a parents' evening when I'd mouthed off at one of the teachers. Offered to get me a cup of coffee—only I wasn't having any of it—

RUBY: I don't blame you.

MAGGIE: /Because I was pissed. And that's the thing about being pissed —you can't see that the way you're behaving is out of order.

Pause.

RUBY: Did you come round to drop off the key Maggie or did you just want to give me a lecture?

MAGGIE: *(laughs)* God, no—I'm the last person in the world qualified to lecture anyone about drinking, aren't I?

RUBY: You're not that bad are you?

MAGGIE: I was—and I'd hate to see you going the same way I did.

RUBY: Give it a rest will you, Maggie.

MAGGIE: Can you remember the last time you had a day without drinking?

RUBY shrugs.

Do you think you could—have a few days off? Might do you the world of good?

RUBY: I dunno.

MAGGIE: Maybe you could just try and stop for a week—see how that goes?

RUBY: A week? Without drinking. Jeez—what am I supposed to do with myself if I can't have a drink? Plus it's my birthday next Saturday—there's no way I can stop drinking before that.

MAGGIE: There'll always be a reason not to stop.

RUBY: Did you actually want anything, Maggie? Or have you just come round here to make my life a misery?

MAGGIE: Oh, I don't think you need any help with that my love.

She goes to leave but then stops and turns back.

You know, I think we're quite alike, you and I—

RUBY: I'm nothing like you!

MAGGIE: Aren't you? I think the only difference is that you can take control of this now.

Pause.

She takes a pen and receipt out of her bag—writes on the back of it.

Look, if you do decide that you want to take a break—and it's too hard to do on your own—then, well, I'm writing my number down here for you. Don't be afraid to use it, will you?

MAGGIE exits.

RUBY picks up the piece of paper and considers for a second, before she screws it up.

SCENE 17: THE NIGGLE (PART TWO)

MAGGIE: Cos you know. Deep down you know

RUBY: That it's not good to be

ALL: counting down the hours until you can have a drink

CALLUM : To be thinking of days out that might involve a glass of wine

MAGGIE: A nice walk with a detour en route for a freshly pulled pint or

RUBY: better still, a cold glass of white or a smooth red as a reward

CALLUM: And when the hangovers start to eat into the days

MAGGIE: you laugh it off as just 'getting older'—stock up on Alka -Seltzer and take one every morning just to clear the fog when

RUBY: BANG! There it is again—

ALL: the niggle

CALLUM: And worse still

RUBY: when you wake up with NO recollection of the last hour of the last night

MAGGIE: It plants a seed and it starts to grow—no longer just a niggle

RUBY: /but a bloody great big bell that you can't silence because

ALL: you're not stupid

CALLUM: Finally, when you don't want to admit

RUBY: that the thought of not having any in the house fills you with a sense of panic

ALL: which you push down and swallow

RUBY: Finally, when you know that you can't ignore it any longer.

CALLUM: You face the facts

MAGGIE: Head on now

RUBY: and you start to unpick the niggle

RUBY stares at the scrunched up piece of paper for a long time, then slowly picks it up and starts to open it……

END

ALCOHOL SUPPORT SERVICES IN THE NORTH WEST

Change Grow Live (Sefton)

CGL has two in-person drug and alcohol services in Sefton—one takes place in Southport and the other in Bootle.

Phone: 0151 203 9755 Email: Sefton.Services@cgl.org.uk

Change Grow Live (North & Central Lancashire)

Have a family support service for people impacted by a loved one's alcohol or substance misuse. A team of family coaches with lived experience, will provide support and information.

Email: northfamilysupport@emergingfutures.org.uk

Change Grow Live (Manchester)

Work with adults, young people and anyone looking to access support. You can attend one of the walk-in sessions if you are an adult over 25 years old.

To make a referral for yourself or someone else, phone: 0161 823 6306

Eclypse (Manchester)

A free and confidential service for young people 25 and under in Manchester. They provide support for anyone concerned about their own or somebody else's drug or alcohol use.

Email: eclypsemanchester@cgl.org.uk Phone: 0161 839 2054

Renaissance (Blackpool)

For a direct referral into Drug and/or Alcohol support, please call: 01253 205157 or email HORIZON at hello@horizonblackpool.uk

NATIONAL ALCOHOL SUPPORT SERVICES

National Association of Children of Alcoholics (NACOA)

Providing information, advice and support for anyone affected by a parent's drinking, whether a child, young person or adult.

Phone: 0800 358 3456 (helpline) Email: helpline@nacoa.org.uk

Drink Aware

Support to change your relationship with alcohol—free and confidential chat and lots of resources and useful information on the website.

Phone: 0300 123 1110 (helpline)

Alcohol Change UK

Focuses entirely on reducing alcohol harm, working across the whole range of serious alcohol harms, from mental and physical to societal and economic.

Phone: 020 3907 8480 Email: contact@alcoholchange.org.uk

Alcoholics Anonymous

Meetings all over the UK. Search for your nearest at www.alcoholics-anonymous.org.uk
Phone: 0800 9177 650 (free National Helpline)
Email: help@aamail.org

Young Minds

Helpline: 0808 802 5544

www.youngminds.org.uk

ALSO AVAILABLE FROM SALAMANDER STREET

All Salamander Street plays can be bought in bulk at a discount for performance or study. Contact info@salamanderstreet.com to enquire about performance licenses.

EAT THE RICH (but maybe not me mates x)
by Jade Franks
ISBN: 9781068233449

Witty, provocative and utterly current—a bold exploration of class, privilege and power from one of the UK's most exciting new playwrights.

THE OLIVE BOY
by Ollie Maddigan
ISBN: 9781068233487

Based on his real life story, Ollie Maddigan's Offie-winning solo show introduces The Olive Boy. Forced to change schools and move in with a man he barely knows, The Olive Boy is attempting to stay sane and finally get a real girlfriend.

CARA AND KELLY ARE BEST FRIENDS FOREVER FOR LIFE by Mojola Akinyemi
ISBN: 9781068233418

A darkly comic two-hander that exposes the nastiest sides of teenage girlhood.

HER
by Jennifer Adam
ISBN: 9781068696268

A play about the damaging effects of gender inequality, the truth about consent that asks, how can you be the change you want to see in the world, when you feel like the world is against you?

WORMHOLES by Emily Jupp
ISBN: 9781068696206

A gripping solo play about coercive control, domestic abuse and how the mind finds a way to escape.

www.salamanderstreet.com

www.ingramcontent.com/pod-product-compliance
Lightning Source LLC
La Vergne TN
LVHW050945080826
845145LV00004B/1416
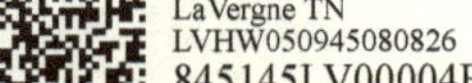

* 9 7 8 1 9 1 9 4 8 3 2 8 3 *